COLOMBIA

The Gateway to South America

GUAJIRA
PENINSULA

Cristóbal Colón peak
(18,947 ft / 5,775 m)

SIERRA NEVADA
OF
SANTA MARTA

Barranquilla

Cartagena

Aracataca

PANAMA

VENEZUELA

Cauca River

Magdalena River

Bucaramanga

Medellín

Cordillera Occidental

Cordillera Central

Oriental

*Pacific
Ocean*

Guatavita

Bogotá

ANDES MOUNTAINS

LLANOS

Cordillera

Neiva

Guaviare River

Popayán

San José del
Guaviare

San Agustín

NARIÑO

Pasto

0°

Equator

ECUADOR

*AMAZON
BASIN*

BRAZIL

PERU

Amazon River

Amazon River

⊙ Capital city

● Major town

▲ Mountain peak

Feet	Meters
10,000	3,050
5,000	1,525
2,000	610
1,000	305
500	152.5
0	0

N

COLOMBIA

0   50   100   150   200 Miles

0   50 100 150 200 Kilometers

CARTO-GRAPHICS

Blackbirch
Exploring World Cultures
Colombia
Size: 35.5p x 53p
CARTO-GRAPHICS

COLOMBIA

The Gateway to South America

Lois Markham

BENCHMARK BOOKS

MARSHALL CAVENDISH

NEW YORK

The publisher would like to thank Linda-Anne Rebhun,
Assistant Professor of Anthropology, Yale University,
for her expert review of the manuscript.

The author wishes to thank Patricia Alvarez and
Connie Restrepo for patiently answering her
many questions about Colombia.

Benchmark Books
Marshall Cavendish Corporation
99 White Plains Road
Tarrytown, New York 10591-9001

© Marshall Cavendish Corporation 1997

Library of Congress Cataloging-in-Publication Data
Markham, Lois.
　　Colombia: The Gateway to South America / by Lois Markham.
　　　　p.　　cm. — (Exploring cultures of the world)
　　Includes bibliographical references and index.
　　Summary: Introduces the geography, history, people, and culture of the country known as the Gateway to South America.
　　ISBN 0-7614-0140-7
　　1. Colombia—Juvenile literature.　[1. Colombia.]　I. Title.　II. Series.
　　F2258.5.M37　　　1997
　　986.1—dc21
　　　　　　　　　　　　　　　　　　　　　　　　　　　96-51580
　　　　　　　　　　　　　　　　　　　　　　　　　　　CIPxx
　　　　　　　　　　　　　　　　　　　　　　　　　　　AC

Printed in Hong Kong

Series design by Carol Matsuyama

Front cover: Young girls dressed in traditional clothes for a folk festival
Back cover: Cathedral on bridge

Photo Credits
Front cover and pages 10, 13, 16, 18, 22, 25, 27, 29, 35, 51, 53: ©Craig Duncan/DDB Stock Photo; back cover: ©Sipa/Brenton/Leo de Wys; title page and page 33: ©Yoram Lehmann/Peter Arnold, Inc.; pages 6, 50: ©Chip and Rosa María de la Cueva Peterson; page 9: ©Alan Cave/DDB Stock Photo; pages 11, 30: ©Victor Englebert/Photo Researchers, Inc.; pages 14, 20, 28, 34, 40, 47: ©John Curtis/DDB Stock Photo; page 15: North Wind Picture Archives; page 17: ©Giraudon/Art Resource, NY; pages 37, 44–45, 57: O. Louis Mazzatenta/National Geographic Image Collection; pages 38, 48: ©Robin J. Dunitz/DDB Stock Photo; page 54: ©Art Resource, NY

Contents

Today a reservoir covers the site of Lake Guatavita, where the Golden Man once floated on a raft.

1
GEOGRAPHY AND HISTORY

Colombia: Land of Seacoasts and Mountains

The Golden Man

Once, high in the Andes Mountains of Colombia, there was a dark, moon-shaped lake called Guatavita. Long, long ago, around dancing fires, the Chibcha Indians, who lived on the shores of the lake, told this story of the Golden Man:

At the bottom of Lake Guatavita lies a mighty serpent. His scales are as green as emeralds. His eyes are ruby red. Once upon a time, this fearsome serpent rose to the surface of the lake, seized the king's wife and daughter, and carried them below to live with him. The king, who loved his family greatly, was grief-stricken by their loss.

At the next full moon, all the Chibcha went to the shores of Lake Guatavita. The high priest prayed to the gods for a sign from the serpent. Suddenly, the full moon disappeared in mist. Strong winds churned the surface of the lake. When the mists cleared, the high priest spoke. "The serpent says that your wife and daughter are happy in his palace. Some day you will join them, but now is not the time. Your people need you. You must rule them wisely."

The king did as he was told, but he was afraid that the serpent would forget its promise. So, once each year, the king had himself covered with fragrant oils and coated with gold dust. He became a Golden Man.

Going down to the shores of Lake Guatavita, he boarded a raft that was laden with gold and emeralds. While flutes played, the king drifted on the raft to the center of the lake. There he tossed the precious cargo into the lake, piece by piece, all the while praying to the serpent to protect his wife and child. When the king had thrown all of the gold and emeralds into the lake, he jumped in himself. The gold dust covering his body washed off in the water.

As millions of tiny gold particles disappeared beneath the surface of the lake, the king swam back to shore. For years this annual ceremony took place. Meanwhile, the king ruled the Chibcha wisely, bringing them peace and prosperity.

One year, at the end of the ceremony, the serpent appeared near the surface of the water. Finally, it had come to keep its promise to the king. Down, down the two traveled. At last they reached the serpent's palace, and the king was reunited with his wife and daughter for all time.

The Chibcha have never forgotten their beloved king. And even today, each new Chibcha king performs the ceremony of the Golden Man so that the serpent will keep the Chibcha kingdom safe.

In the early 1500s, when Spanish explorers first arrived in the land now called Colombia, the Indians told them the story of the Golden Man—*El Dorado*, in Spanish. Like all legends, this one was changed a little as it passed from person to person. Eventually, El Dorado was thought to be a city or a kingdom of gold. Many Spanish explorers eagerly sought

El Dorado. Some even cut a wedge into the side of Lake Guatavita, hoping to drain it and find the gold at the bottom of the lake. But the lake quickly filled up again, and no one has yet found the riches of El Dorado.

The Four Colombias

Would you like to visit the mountains? How about a trip to the seashore? Want to ride on the plains with cowboys? Or is a tropical rain forest your idea of an interesting place? You can find all of these things in Colombia. The country has four very different land areas, providing homes for a great variety of plants and animals. In fact, Colombia has more different kinds of plants and animals than any other nation in the world except Brazil.

Mountains are one of Colombia's most distinctive features. The Andes Mountains, which stretch loftily along the western regions of South America, form the backbone of Colombia. Just after the Andes chain enters Colombia from Ecuador in the south, it splits into three ranges that run north

Brightly colored birds like the toucan live in the lush Colombian rain forest.

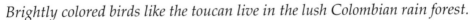

and south. These are the Cordillera Occidental (western), the Cordillera Central (middle), and the Cordillera Oriental (eastern). *Cordillera* (kor-dee-YEH-rah) means "mountain range" in Spanish. The Occidental and Central Cordilleras drop down to the coasts, while the Oriental stretches into Venezuela. The valleys of two rivers—the Magdalena and the Cauca—separate the three ranges. Most Colombians live in the mountains and their valleys, in high, flat areas called plateaus.

Colombia has two separate seacoasts. The Pacific Ocean coast lies west of the Andes. The land gradually descends to a narrow plain that borders the wild sea. Marshlands and

Like a patchwork quilt, farmers' fields blanket the rolling hills of the Cordillera Occidental.

Cowboys round up cattle in the broad, flat llanos.

dense tropical rain forests cover this plain. North of the Andes region, the Caribbean coastal plain leads to the tranquil shore of the Caribbean Sea. This plain is broken only by one twin peaked mountain, called the Sierra Nevada of Santa Marta. Its Cristóbal Colón peak is the highest point in Colombia. It soars 18,947 feet (5,775 meters) high. The hot, dry Guajira Peninsula, consisting mainly of salt flats, forms the easternmost section of the Caribbean coast. It is bordered by Venezuela.

About 60 percent of Colombia lies east of the Andes Mountains, but this vast expanse of land holds only about 2 percent of the country's population. This area is divided into two different regions. In the north are the llanos (YAH-nos), or plains. These grasslands have poor soil, but they are well suited to grazing cattle. The discovery of rich petroleum deposits in 1984 brought new economic development to the llanos. South of the llanos is the steamy Amazon Basin, a huge area covered by humid tropical rain forests. The massive, mysterious Amazon River forms a small section of the southern border of Colombia. In this area, Colombia, Peru, and Brazil all come together on the banks of the Amazon.

From Bathing Suits to Snowsuits

If you want to explore Colombia, you'll need to pack clothing for many different kinds of climates—from humid beach weather to hot plains to cool mountain air. Because Colombia lies on the equator—the invisible line separating the Northern and Southern Hemispheres—the sun strikes it at the same angle all year long. Thus, the temperatures in each region do not change very much over the course of the year. Still, temperatures vary a great deal from region to region, depending on the area's height above sea level. The lowlands have a hot, moist climate. High up in the mountains, it is so cool that some of the peaks are snow-capped all year long. The Pacific coast of Colombia is one of the rainiest areas of the world. It rains there almost every day. Other regions of the country have distinct wet and dry seasons during the year.

A Country of Cities

Colombia's capital is Bogotá (bow-go-TAH), one of the oldest cities in all the Americas. Located in a high valley of the Andes, it has a pleasant, springlike climate throughout the year. The old city, centered around the cathedral and a square called the Plaza Bolívar, is full of narrow streets. Two-storied buildings with red-tile roofs and carved wooden balconies line the streets. Around this quaint central core, a new city of tall, modern buildings has arisen. More than 5 million people live in Bogotá, and more arrive every day from the countryside, looking for jobs. There are so many people that Bogotá is bursting at the seams, and many of these newcomers end up living in crowded slums.

Colombia is a very urban country. Besides Bogotá, there are thirty-two cities with populations over 100,000!

Clock towers grace buildings in a historic district of Bogotá.

The First Colombians

Thousands of years ago, the first Americans traveled from the Asian continent across a land bridge that once connected present-day Siberia with Alaska. From there, they slowly moved south, peopling the vast continent. Possibly as early as 20,000 B.C., these Native Americans arrived in South America, in what is now Colombia. Almost nothing is known of these first settlers. Around 1200 B.C., another group of Indians arrived from Central America. These people knew how to grow corn. Between 400 and 300 B.C., the Chibcha (CHEEB-cha), also called the Muisca (moo-EES-kah), migrated, or moved, to Colombia. They came from the Central American countries now known as Nicaragua and Honduras.

13

This man is harvesting corn much the way his Indian ancestors did centuries ago.

By A.D. 1500, there were two main Indian groups: the Chibcha and the Tairona (tie-ROW-nah). The Chibcha lived in the plateaus near what is now Bogotá. There they grew potatoes, corn, and other crops. They had a highly developed civilization. It has been compared to those of the Maya, the Aztecs, and the Incas— all very sophisticated societies.

The Tairona lived on both the coast of the Guajira Peninsula and on the slopes of the Sierra Nevada of Santa Marta, the twin-peaked mountain. People on the coast fished and harvested salt. Those living in the highlands produced cotton cloth and blankets. These two groups of Tairona traded with each other. Both groups lived in towns connected by stone roads. Remnants of some of these old roads can still be seen today.

Invaders and Colonizers

Colombia is named for Christopher Columbus. But the Italian explorer, funded by Spain, never saw that land. In 1499, seven years after Columbus's first voyage to the Americas, the Spanish explorer Alonso de Ojeda landed in what is now Colombia. Rodrigo de Bastidas established the first permanent Spanish settlement, at Santa Marta, on the Caribbean coast, in 1525. Over the next years, the Spanish built several more towns along the Caribbean.

Through their encounters with the Tairona Indians, the Spanish became convinced that there was gold on the South American continent. In 1536, Gonzalo Jiménez de Quesada led an expedition up the alligator-infested Magdalena River, hoping to find a golden treasure. There, he met the Chibcha in the plateaus of the Cordillera Oriental. It was a violent meeting. Jiménez de Quesada and his men, with their superior weapons, defeated the Chibcha. Jiménez de Quesada founded the city of Bogotá in 1538. And the area that today is known as Colombia was named New Granada, for a city in Spain. The region had become a Spanish colony.

The Spanish seized all the Chibcha treasures they could find. Then they forced the Indians to work in gold and emerald mines to unearth yet more wealth for Spain. Many Indians died from the harsh treatment. Others lost their lives to such diseases as measles and influenza. They had never before been exposed to these diseases and therefore had no immunity to them. Thousands died. Many of the surviving Indians intermarried with Spanish settlers. In a very short time, Colombia's Indian cultures and languages had all

Gonzalo Jiménez de Quesada, the conquistador who founded the city of Bogotá

More emeralds are found in Colombia than anywhere else in the world. These are rough, uncut gems.

but died out. Only small groups of Indians living in areas that were remote or of little interest to the Spanish survived.

With the Indian population greatly reduced, the Spanish needed to find new sources of labor. They began importing enslaved Africans to work in the mines and plantations. The gold, silver, emeralds, and other precious stones that workers dug out of the mines were sent to the coastal towns, to be shipped to Spain. Cartagena especially became an important shipping center—and a magnet for greedy pirates.

A New Nation

For almost three centuries, Spaniards who came to New Granada from Spain held most of the power in the colony. Creoles—people of Spanish ancestry who were born in New Granada—did not like this. Thus, starting in the 1780s, more and more Creoles supported a movement for independence from Spain. Eventually, Creoles assumed power and issued an Act of Independence on July 20, 1810. While the act pledged New Granada's loyalty to the Spanish king, it claimed greater self-government for the colony. Today, Colombians celebrate July 20 as their country's Independence Day.

Freedom was not to be won simply with the stroke of a pen, however. Spain forcibly took control of the colony again in 1814. A group of rebels led by Francisco de Paula Santander escaped to the llanos, the flat lands in the east. There they joined forces with the Venezuelan leader Simón Bolívar.

Today, Bolívar is known as the "George Washington of South America." He helped win independence for Colombia, Venezuela, Panama, Ecuador, Peru, and Bolivia.

The combined forces of Santander and Bolívar defeated the Spanish at Boyacá on August 7, 1819. Colombia's first Constitution was adopted in 1821. The new nation was called Gran ("Great") Colombia. Until 1830, this republic included Venezuela, Ecuador, and Panama, as well as Colombia. In 1830, Venezuela and Ecuador withdrew from Gran Colombia. Panama did so in 1903.

In the 1800s, Colombians split into two opposing political groups: the Conservatives and the Liberals. The Conservatives favored a strong central government, solid ties between the government and the Catholic Church, and limited voting rights. The Liberals wanted to extend voting rights to more people, give more power to local government, and keep church and state separate. These groups gave rise to two political parties that still exist today. The Constitution of 1886 favored the Conservative position. Although it has been amended (changed) several times, this Constitution is still the basis of Colombia's government.

Simón Bolívar, the "George Washington of South America"

Into the Twentieth Century

In the late 1800s, conflict arose between Colombia and the United States. The United States wanted to build a canal across Panama, a channel cut across the land that would join the Atlantic and Pacific Oceans. When Colombia refused to allow this, the United States encouraged Panama to declare its independence from Gran Colombia. After a successful rebellion, Panama did so, and the new nation welcomed the building of the Panama Canal.

The first thirty years of the century were a time of economic growth for Colombia. A textile industry developed, and coffee beans became an important export. Still, many of Colombia's people were very poor. Most of the land was owned by a few rich people, and many peasants, or poor farmers, worked it. In the 1930s, a president from the Liberal Party made a series of important changes, and some progress was made toward making life more fair for all the people.

A popular Liberal Party politician was killed by an opponent in 1948. This set off a civil war—one of the most violent periods in Colombia's history. Over the next ten years, more than 200,000 people were killed in widespread fighting. Liberals fought Conservatives. The poor attacked the rich. Those in support of the

This coffee farmer rakes ripe beans on burlap sheets so they can dry in the sun.

COLOMBIAN GOVERNMENT

Colombia is a republic and is divided into thirty-three departments (somewhat like U.S. states) and other districts. The central government has three branches. The executive branch is headed by a president, who is elected by the people for a four-year term. The legislative branch consists of two bodies: the House of Representatives, with 163 members; and the Senate, with 102 seats, two of which must be filled by Indian communities. Members of both houses are elected to four-year terms. The judicial branch, headed by the Supreme Court of twenty judges, also includes various district tribunals and lower courts.

According to the Colombian Constitution, citizens have certain rights. These include freedom of education, freedom of the press, and the right to strike (except in government-run organizations).

Catholic Church did battle with those who opposed it. This period is known as *La Violencia* ("The Violence").

By 1957, some Liberal and Conservative politicians believed they could save their country from destruction only by working together. To this end, they created the National Front, a political organization that restored peace to Colombia.

In recent years, other forces have threatened Colombia's well-being. There is still a strong division between rich and poor. Armed rebels called "guerrillas" make war throughout the country, claiming that their goal is to bring about economic reforms, or changes. The government has encouraged the guerrillas to work *within* the government to improve life for the poor. This effort has had some success.

Another major threat to Colombia's peace is drug traffickers. These criminals use Colombia as a shipping center for cocaine, a drug that is made from coca leaves, which are grown all over the Andes. They do not hesitate to kill and kidnap to protect their illegal operations. However, many Colombians bravely oppose them—in another struggle to bring peace and justice to their country.

This young man of Indian ancestry, wearing a warm hat and a ruana, lives high in the mountains of western Colombia.

2

THE PEOPLE

The Many Faces of Colombia

What do the Kogi *mamas* have in common with the world-famous novelist Gabriel García Márquez and the *zambos* of the Caribbean coast? They are Colombians all! Come meet some of the many different people who call Colombia home.

From Three Continents

Today's Colombians trace their roots to three different continents. Some are Indians, whose ancestors migrated to the Americas thousands of years ago. Some are the direct descendants of Africans brought to South America as slaves. Others find their ancestry in the white Europeans, mostly Spanish, who colonized the land. But by far the greatest percentage of Colombia's population are of mixed heritage.

The largest single group of Colombians—about 58 percent of the population—are mestizo, mixed Indian and white. Another 20 percent are white, mostly of Spanish heritage.

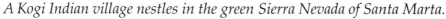

Seventeen percent are either mulatto (mixed black and white) or *zambo* (mixed black and Indian). About 4 percent of the Colombian people today are black, and about 1 percent are pure Indian.

Native Heritage

Though most of Colombia's Indians have been absorbed into Colombia's modern culture, some groups have kept themselves apart. The Kogi are one of them.

The Kogi make their home in the Sierra Nevada of Santa Marta mountain in northern Colombia. They are descendants of the Tairona, who inhabited the Sierra Nevada and the nearby Caribbean coast when the Spanish settlers first arrived. Under attack from the Spanish, those Tairona who

A Kogi Indian village nestles in the green Sierra Nevada of Santa Marta.

could fled up the mountain, leaving behind their gold and other precious objects. The Spanish didn't consider the mountain worth fighting for, so they left the fugitives alone. For close to 500 years, the Kogi have avoided contact with the outside world.

Today, they still follow a lifestyle similar to that of their Tairona ancestors. They no longer have the gold and emerald objects that were once part of their religious ceremonies. But the Kogi are rich in the life of the spirit. In all matters they are guided by priests, called *mamas*. The *mamas* undergo a rigorous training from childhood to prepare them for their religious duties. The Kogi believe in the sacredness of nature and in the connection between nature and human beings. They call themselves the "Elder Brothers" and the rest of us the "Younger Brothers of Mother Earth."

In recent years, the Elder Brothers have noticed alarming changes in their natural environment caused by the thoughtless behavior of the Younger Brothers. To save themselves, the earth, and the Younger Brothers, the Kogi allowed a film to be made at some of their villages. After speaking about their beliefs on film, however, they insisted that they wanted no more contact with the Younger Brothers. The Kogi have spoken. They hope that the rest of us will pay attention to their message.

Similarities and Differences

Despite their different backgrounds, 95 percent of Colombians have one thing in common: they are Roman Catholics. Most practice only Catholicism. Some, however, combine Catholicism with parts of the Indian or African religions of their ancestors. Some Indians follow only their traditional

SAY IT IN SPANISH

Here is how you would say some common words and phrases in Spanish.

Hi!	*¡Hola!* (OH-lah)
How are you?	*¿Cómo está usted?* (COH-moh es-TAH oo-STEHD)
I'm fine.	*Estoy bien.* (ehs-TOY bee-EHN)
Good morning.	*Buenos días.* (BWAY-nohs DEE-ahs)
Please.	*Por favor.* (pohr fah-VOHR)
Thank you.	*Gracias.* (GRAH-see-ahs)
What's going on?	*¿Qué pasa?* (keh PAH-sah)

Uno (OO-noh), *dos* (dohs), *tres* (trays), *cuatro* (KUAH-troh), *cinco* (SEEN-coh), *seis* (SEHS), *siete* (see-EH-teh), *ocho* (OH-choh), *nueve* (noo-EH-veh), *diez* (dee-EHZ): one, two, three, four, five, six, seven, eight, nine, ten.

religions. Colombia is also home to a small number of Jews and a growing number of Protestants.

The Spanish language is another strong unifying force in Colombia. Except for some Indians in isolated areas, most Colombians speak Spanish.

While most Colombians are united in religion and language, they are deeply divided by income and education levels. A small fraction of them are wealthy, and about one fifth earn a comfortable living. However, about half of Colombia's people fall into a category called the working poor; they have jobs but make barely enough money to get by. And fully one quarter of Colombians are extremely poor. They have little or no education and almost no hope of improving their standard of living.

City Dwellers

Tall buildings of steel and glass, bustling streets alive with jostling crowds and honking horns—Colombia's cities are like cities the world over. Seventy-three percent of Colombians live in cities, a high number of urban dwellers. They earn their living like city dwellers elsewhere. Some are bankers, lawyers, teachers, or government workers. Some work in shops that sell local products such as textiles, emeralds, leather goods, and handicrafts. Others find jobs in local industries. They make tires and chemical products in Bogotá or manufacture textiles in Medellín, the nation's second largest city.

In recent years, many people have moved to the cities from the countryside, hoping to improve their lives. Few have been able to do so, however. Many have difficulty finding jobs. Some set up small stalls in the street. They earn a meager living selling odds and ends like shoelaces or sweets. Children may help out by doing odd jobs like washing cars or polishing shoes.

Busy street scenes such as this one in Medellín are a common sight in many of Colombia's cities.

Life is hard for the newcomers. The cities were not prepared to supply services for so many people. They have not been able to provide adequate housing, schools, or health care for many of their new residents. Many of the newcomers end up living in crowded shantytowns, neighborhoods of shacks. They often have no running water or electricity.

In contrast, wealthy Colombians live in lovely residential areas. Their homes often have swimming pools and beautifully kept lawns and gardens. Middle-class city dwellers live comfortably in modest brick or concrete houses or apartments. But there is a shortage of this kind of housing as well.

Many Different Countrysides

Colombians who do not live in cities have a wide variety of lifestyles, depending on what kind of natural environment they live in.

On the slopes of the Andes, agriculture is the main occupation. Coffee is an especially important crop. It thrives in the humid climate at high elevations. Coffee trees are grown mainly on small farms that are owned or rented by families. The berries must be picked by hand. During the harvest season, three generations of a family may work in the fields from sunup to sundown. One tree may yield about 2,000 berries—enough, when processed, to fill only a one-pound can of coffee. Coffee growing is hard work, but coffee growers enjoy a better standard of living than most other Colombians.

Other common Andean agricultural products include sugarcane, rice, cotton, tobacco, soybeans, and various fruits. In the countryside near Medellín, orchids are grown to be sold to the United States. And on a treeless plain near Bogotá,

26

On a road in southwestern Colombia, wagons loaded with cut sugarcane make their way to market.

many more kinds of flowers are grown for export to other countries.

In some mountain towns, mud or stone houses of one or two stories have red roofs. Inside, all the rooms open onto a courtyard filled with flowers. The family gathers there to relax and eat. East of the mountains, the llanos are wild frontier territory, good for raising cattle and growing grain. Colombian cowboys, called *llaneros* (yah-NAI-rohs), sit in the saddle all day keeping track of the large herds.

The Caribbean and Pacific coasts are dotted with many small fishing villages. Lush banana plantations take up some of the land near the Caribbean coast.

In the Amazonian rain forest, an Indian fashions a sturdy roof for his home out of leaves.

The tropical rain forest of the Amazon region offers yet another way of life. The Indians there hunt and fish to provide food for themselves and their families. Their homes are often raised platforms with thatched roofs. This unusual design keeps them from being flooded. The sides are open and people get wet when it rains, but the heat dries things quickly.

Dressing Up, Dressing Down

Colombia does not have a national dress. City dwellers wear modern-style clothes, just like those worn by people in North America and Europe. The size of the city determines the formality of the dress, however. In Bogotá, the capital, people dress more formally, and even wear fancy clothes.

In the countryside, dress is more casual. A popular garment is the ruana (roo-AH-nuh). It is a woolen cloak with a hole in the middle for the head. The ruana comes to just below the knees. The natural oils in the wool yarns make the ruanas waterproof. When not being worn, a ruana is folded and carried over one shoulder. Among poorer Colombians, the ruana also serves as a blanket.

Another common article of clothing is the black derby-style hat. Round on the top with a narrow brim, these hats are worn by men, women, and children alike.

Wearing a ruana and a derby-style hat, an Indian woman quietly spins wool thread.

Each of Colombia's Indian groups also has its own special kinds of clothes. In the hot rain forest, clothing is kept to a minimum. But the Kogi, who live on a mountainside, dress for cool weather. Kogi men wear simple trousers and shirts of homespun cotton. Kogi women wear tunics of the same material. Only the *mamas*—the spiritual leaders—are allowed to wear woven hats that come to a point. Other Kogi men wear hats that are braided into a circular shape.

Several generations of Colombians gather for a family portrait.

3

FAMILY LIFE, FESTIVALS, AND FOOD

Traditional Ways

If you ask a Colombian child to name family members, you will probably get a long list. That's because when Colombians think of family, they think not only of parents and brothers and sisters, but also of grandparents, aunts, uncles, cousins, and even more relatives.

A family in which many relatives are involved in one another's lives on a regular basis is called an extended family. In Colombia, members of extended families see one another often. Cousins play together after school. Aunts and uncles may drop by each other's homes after work for a short visit. Grandparents may live nearby or in the same household with their grandchildren.

Extended families give Colombians many close emotional ties. They are also important in political and business activities. Extended family members help one another out in any way they can. If someone is looking for a new job, for example, a family member may know of an opportunity.

Extended families are still a way of life for many Colombians. However, some have given up the security of the extended family to move to a city in search of a better life. Unfortunately, often the new city dweller has neither a better life nor an extended family to turn to for help.

One Child, Many Parents

Most Colombian families are made even larger by the custom of giving each child at least two godparents. For many Christians, "godparents" are friends or members of the family who agree to look after the spiritual well-being of a child. In Colombia, however, godparents have more than a religious role. They have a very close relationship with their godchild. This special relationship continues even after the child becomes an adult. In a way, godparents are part of a person's extended family.

Colombian children may have more than one set of godparents. But the most important are the ones chosen when an infant is baptized in the Catholic faith. Other godparents may be chosen at other special events in a person's life.

Godparents are close to the parents as well as the child. To the child, the godmother and godfather are *madrina* and *padrino*. To the parents, they are *comadre* and *compadre*— "co-mother" and "co-father." This relationship is known as *compadrazgo*—"co-parenting." It suggests that caring for the child is a joint project of several adults.

Family Ways

Traditionally, in well-to-do Colombian families, the father is the authority figure. He provides for the family financially. When important decisions need to be made, he makes them for the whole family. He considers it his responsibility to protect his family.

A mother in rural Colombia serves her family a meal first before eating herself.

The mother's role is to raise the children and take care of the household. In families with a good income, the mother usually has one or two paid servants to help with the cooking and cleaning.

In recent years, more women from wealthy families have taken jobs outside of the home. Women from less prosperous families have always needed to work outside of the home to earn money for their families.

Fiesta!

Colombians work hard. Many are at their jobs six days a week, with Sunday their only day off. They do, however, enjoy celebrating many holidays throughout the year. These are called fiesta—festival—days. Fiesta days are a time for parades, fireworks, and dancing in the streets. However, many of the celebrations also have a serious side.

Colombians celebrate eighteen official national holidays a year. Twelve of these are religious holidays associated with the Catholic Church. Since so many Colombians are Catholic, these religious celebrations are observed by most people.

At Christmas time, people love to get together with family and friends. Parties can go on all night long, with dancing and feasting. People decorate their houses with a tree and nativity scene and give presents to one another.

In the city of Popayán, in southwestern Colombia, the people make a two-day celebration of the end of the Christmas season. The Christmas season comes to an end on January 6, the feast of the Epiphany, when the Three Kings visited the baby Jesus.

Colombians in the city of Cali celebrate Christmas by dancing in the streets.

The day before the Epiphany, January 5, is *El Día de los Negritos* ("The Day of the Black Ones"). Mischievous boys coat their hands with black shoe polish and chase after girls, trying to smear them with the grease. This rowdy behavior comes from an old custom. In the past, men strolling beneath ladies' balconies on this date were allowed to paint a black spot on a lady's cheek or forehead when she appeared at the door. In addition to the silliness, there are parades. People in costumes and masks listen to strolling musicians, eat lots of food, and dance at parties that go on and on.

Gigantic floats draw big crowds in a parade celebrating the Epiphany.

The next day, January 6, is *La Fiesta de los Blanquitos* ("The Festival of the White Ones"). Young people go about with sacks of flour, tossing the white powder on everyone they see. Sometimes, people on balconies pour water on passersby, creating a sticky mess. Many Colombians also take time out to remember the religious meaning of the day.

Carnaval

Not long after the end of the Christmas season, it's time for another period of celebration: *Carnaval* ("Carnival"). It comes before Lent, a solemn, forty-day period before the joyous day of Easter. During Lent, people show their religious faith by giving up certain pleasures, such as candy. But before Lent there is *Carnaval*, the week-long fiesta to say good-bye to pleasures. Nearly all the towns and cities celebrate *Carnaval*, but the most famous one is held in Barranquilla, on the

Caribbean coast. The city's festivities, with parades, floats, and dances, are so wild that they have earned Barranquilla the nickname "the crazy city."

San Isidro

Some fiestas are local. They are celebrated in just one place, rather than throughout the nation. A festival may be held to honor a local patron saint. It also helps to bring together members of a community. One such fiesta is celebrated by the citizens of the town of Río Frío. They mark the end of the dry season with a festival in honor of San Isidro (Saint Isadore the Farmer), who is supposed to bring rain. Each April 4, all of the townspeople parade behind an image of the saint, chanting their need for rain. They hope that San Isidro will send rain before the end of the festival. To make it easier for him to meet their request, they walk very, very slowly— two steps backward for every one forward. If it's not raining after several turns around the town, the chanting turns into scolding. If rain still doesn't come, the celebrants may start to yell at the saint. If that doesn't work, they give up, assuming that rain will come eventually anyhow.

Let's Eat!

In Colombia, food is an important part of fiestas—and of every other day. Colombians eat three meals a day. Breakfast is not a family meal. Each person eats when it is convenient. For example, fathers may have their breakfast and be off to work before the children are even awake. Some Colombians breakfast lightly on fruit, juice, and pastries. Others have a hearty meal of eggs and meat and *arepas*, the corn pancakes that are a national dish.

The midday meal is the most important family meal. Everyone gathers at home for a big hot meal, which may begin around 12:30 or 1:00 P.M. and last until 2:30. Fathers take this break to spend time with their young children, who may be in bed by the time they return home from work in the evening. The meal often begins with soup, followed by meat, rice, and vegetables, and topped off by dessert.

The evening meal is similar to the noon meal. However, there is usually no soup.

Table manners are much as they are in North America, except that it is considered polite to have the left hand visible and above the table at all times. Colombians generally leave a small amount of food on the plate to show that enough was served. Silverware placed across the plate indicates that the person has finished eating.

Grilled meats are the highlight of this special family lunch.

Starchy foods are a big part of the Colombian diet. Potatoes, rice, *arepas*, and manioc (cassava root) are the country's most important foods. Rice is frequently used in making desserts, such as *arroz con coco*, rice cooked with coconut milk.

Colombians eat a great variety of soups and hearty stews. In the Andes, *changua* soup, which is made with beef broth,

Every Wednesday is market day in this mountain village.

AREPAS: A COLOMBIAN FAVORITE

Arepas are cornmeal pancakes—either slim or plump—that are sliced in half like muffins and buttered or filled with cheese, meat, or vegetables. The cornmeal can usually be found in North America in *bodegas*, the small grocery stores that serve Latin American neighborhoods.

    1 cup precooked white cornmeal
    1/2 teaspoon salt
    1 1/2 cups lukewarm water

Stir together the cornmeal and the salt. Slowly add the water and knead the mixture with your hands until it is smooth. Let stand for 5 minutes. Mold the dough into small cakes about 2 1/2 inches across by 1 inch deep. Fry the cakes on both sides in a lightly greased skillet until a crust forms. Then bake them in a 350° F oven for 10 to 15 minutes.

milk, and chopped coriander (an herb), is often served for breakfast. Another popular soup in Colombia is *ajiaco de pollo*. This is made with chicken, vegetables, cream, and avocado. *Sopa de pan*, made from bread, eggs, and cheese, is a hearty main-course stew.

With all the cattle raised on the llanos, meat is popular in Colombia. If the beef is tough, cooks first boil it to make it tender and then roast it to add flavor. Meat is sometimes used as a stuffing for the pastry turnovers called *empanadas*. *Tamales* are another kind of meat pie. In one popular recipe, chopped pork, potatoes, peas, onion, eggs, and olives are wrapped in banana leaves and steamed.

Fruit grows everywhere in Colombia's tropical climate. Besides apples, oranges, and other varieties available in North America, there are also unusual local fruits with names like *maracuya* and *curuba*. All of these may be blended into *jugos*, tasty fresh-fruit drinks.

Students, wearing their school uniforms, proudly wave the Colombian flag.

4
SCHOOL AND RECREATION

School Days, Fun Days

Colombian children get their new school clothes, pencil boxes, and notebooks in February. That is when the school year starts. School is in session from February until the end of June. From the end of June to mid-July, there is a short vacation. Then students go back to school until mid-November, when the longest vacation of the year starts. Since the climate is almost the same year-round, there is no need for a "summer" vacation. Instead, Colombian schools take their long break around the Christmas holidays.

Time to Learn

The Colombian Constitution guarantees every child the right to an education. The government provides free public schooling to all children. However, many well-to-do families prefer to send their children to private schools. Many of these are run by the Catholic Church. Still, the government has authority over all schools, both public and private.

Children between six and fourteen years of age are expected to attend primary school. In the cities, most do. But in the countryside, attendance is not as regular. This is because parents sometimes must keep children out of school in order to work and help support the family.

Even those who can afford to let their children go to school sometimes find that getting them there is a problem. Schools in the country are few and far between. Students may have to travel great distances to get to school, and not many families have their own cars.

Students who complete primary school may go on to attend high school. Most high schools are located in urban areas, so few rural youngsters attend them. Almost half of the secondary schools are private. Those students who do well in high school may continue their education at a university. There are dozens of institutions of higher learning in Colombia. Most of these are in the major cities.

In the Classroom

School hours depend somewhat on the climate. In warmer areas, for example, students start early in the morning and finish by early afternoon. It is not unusual for students to be at their desks by 7:30 A.M.

Colombian youngsters study the same subjects as students in North America do—social studies, math, and science. Of course, their language class is Spanish. English is taught in some primary schools. It is the main foreign language taught in high schools.

At least once a month, students attend a special civics assembly to show respect for their country. They sing the Colombian national anthem and pledge allegiance to the flag. A group of students may put on a play about whatever holiday is coming up next.

In the Jungle

In the Amazon, Indian children whose parents still practice their traditional ways of life may have a very different kind of education. There is no formal schooling. Instead, children carefully observe the adults around them, watching how they accomplish the various tasks that keep the community going.

To outsiders, it sometimes looks as if these children—the boys especially—are not doing anything, for they may be silent and inactive for long periods. Then, one day, a boy begins to imitate what he has seen his father do. It may be fishing, hunting, or gathering plants for medicine. In a remarkably short time, the boy himself has become skilled at it, through observation and practice. He has finished his schooling in this "subject."

School's Out!

When school ends for the day, Colombian children race home to play—often with cousins from their extended family. Children from well-to-do city families have many of the same toys that are available in North America. However, board games are not as widely available.

Computer games are also not very common in Colombia. Parents want their children out in the fresh air, so they are less likely to buy things that will keep kids inside.

When they play outside, children are likely to gather their friends together for a game of soccer—a national craze—or find a spot to go swimming.

In the countryside, fewer toys are available, and there is not as much money to be spent on them. Still, children might have wooden trucks, cars, and boats. If the family is doing well financially, they might have a tricycle or bicycle.

Everyone in Colombia loves soccer, called fútbol. *Here, children in Cartagena practice on the street.*

Colombian youngsters play the same games that children enjoy everywhere: hide-and-go-seek, hopscotch, and marbles. They also like to fly kites and jump rope.

One popular game in Colombia is *Juan Palmada* ("Johnny Clap-Hands"). In this game, children sit in a circle. One spot is left empty. Two children stand back-to-back outside the circle, just behind the empty spot. At a signal, they start to run around the circle in opposite directions. When they meet, they must jump up and clap their hands together over their heads. Then they continue running. The first one to reach the empty spot claims it. Then the person to the right stands up and the game continues.

Fun for All

Children aren't the only Colombians who enjoy leisure time. On Sundays and holidays, adults also take time out for fun.

TEJO

*T*ejo (TAY-ho) is a popular traditional game. Almost every Colombian town has a *tejo* court. However, the rules of play may differ from place to place.

Two metal pipes are set in the ground about forty feet (twelve meters) apart. Dirt is heaped around each pipe until it is nearly covered. The tops of the pipes are loaded with a small amount of gunpowder (*mecha*).

Players take turns throwing the *tejo*—a smooth, rounded piece of metal or stone—at the loaded pipe. When it hits, there is a loud explosive sound. Onlookers shout encouragement at the best players, who can trigger the *mecha* with great regularity.

As with so many things in Colombia, what you do for fun depends on where you live. On the two coastlines, water sports are popular. A day off is often spent at the beach, swimming, snorkeling, fishing, surfing, or waterskiing.

Many people who live in the mountains like to spend their free time hiking and enjoying the scenery. Often a large group of family members and friends will spend a whole day on mountain trails. They will take time out for a picnic lunch and perhaps find a quiet pond or stream to cool off in.

For organized sports, there's no doubt what is *numero uno*—"number one." Like most Latin Americans, Colombians prefer soccer above all else. Baseball and basketball do, however, have their share of fans. Colombia also regularly sends players to international table-tennis competitions.

Every major city in Colombia has a *plaza de toros*, or bullring. Early Spanish settlers brought bullfighting from Spain to Colombia, and Colombians still flock to watch the

The turtle pool at the oceanarium in Cartagena draws crowds all year long.

bullfights. Colombia sometimes hosts international bull-fighting festivals. Matadors (bullfighters) go there from all over the world.

Throughout the year, on Thursday and Sunday afternoons, daring matadors, dressed in dazzling costumes, perform graceful passes with their capes to lure the bulls into confrontation. Unless the matador makes a serious mistake, the matador wins and the bull is killed. Today, many people see bullfighting as a cruel practice. But in Colombia, it is a tradition, and Colombia is a country that respects its traditions.

47

Embroidery is an ancient craft in Colombia. This beautiful piece shows life in a mountain village.

5

THE ARTS

One Nation, Many Arts

Some of Colombia's art is ancient, and some is as fresh as tomorrow. Today's craftspeople still make beautiful objects in gold, stone, clay, textiles, and wood. Newer traditions, developed in the last 500 years, include painting on canvas and written literature. Music and dance are as old as the land but are constantly finding new ways of expression.

Of Gold and Stones

It is no wonder that the Spanish conquistadores believed the legend of El Dorado. When they arrived in Colombia, some 500 years ago, they found Indians using golden fish hooks, needles, and tweezers for everyday activities. Larger gold items had both practical and ceremonial use. Helmets and breastplates, for example, were used both for protection in battle and to indicate one's status in ceremonies.

Driven by gold fever, the Spanish looted graves and burned villages. They carried away as much Indian gold as they could.

This beautiful gold work of art depicts the raft of El Dorado.

Still, some of it escaped their notice. Today, you can see about 35,000 gold objects from pre-Columbian days in Bogota's Gold Museum. (The term "pre-Columbian" refers to the days before the Europeans came to the Americas.) Jewelry, musical instruments, spoons, and bowls fill the rooms of the museum. More important than their monetary value is what they tell of long-ago peoples and of the sophisticated methods they developed for working with gold.

One of the objects in the Gold Museum is a miniature golden replica of El Dorado's raft. On that raft, Chibcha leaders floated to the middle of Lake Guatavita to toss a king's ransom to the bottom of the lake.

Not all of Colombia's ancient treasures are in a museum. Some are right out in plain sight of all passersby, but no one can steal them. They are too big. Such treasures are found in a place that, today, is called San Agustín. In 1757, a Spanish monk traveling along the Magdalena River happened upon the remains of a very old Indian civilization. Hundreds of huge stone carvings representing animals, monsters, and humans filled the area. Archaeologists—scientists who study ancient peoples and their cultures—are still not sure of the meaning of these carvings. Some believe that they had religious meaning.

Yesterday's Traditions Today

Gold is still mined in Colombia, and some Colombians still create beautiful works out of the precious metal. Others work in other traditional art forms, such as ceramics (pottery).

Colombian pottery is offered for sale at an outdoor market in a village in the mountains.

Ancient ceramic objects have been found all over Colombia. The oldest, found on the northern coast, date back to about 3500 B.C. Indian potters made both practical and ceremonial items. They shaped clay into adobe bricks for building. They made ceramic pots, pitchers, and cups for everyday use. These might be decorated with mythical or religious pictures, or left completely plain. Clay was also used to make whistles, flutes, panpipes, and other musical instruments.

The Spanish colonists introduced new pottery techniques, including high-temperature kilns, or ovens, for firing pottery, new methods of decoration, and the potter's wheel. Today's Colombian potters—mostly women, as in the past—use a mixture of ancient and modern techniques to create their wares. Many pieces are glazed. Some potters use the ancient technique of burnishing—repeatedly rubbing a pot with stones—before firing it. The ceramics made today range from practical kitchen bowls to such fun items as piggy banks shaped like hens. Decorative pieces may represent Christmas scenes or show wedding parties perched atop crowded buses.

Woven in Time

Weaving is another of Colombia's arts. The country's climate produces many different kinds of fibers. They can be woven into everything from cotton cloth to baskets. Colombian weaving was well developed before the arrival of the Spanish. However, the newcomers introduced sheep, which added wool to the range of materials available for weaving.

Different areas of Colombia produce different kinds of woven goods. Among farmers and fishers of the Caribbean area, especially the Arhuaco Indians, there is a great demand

It took centuries to perfect the craft of basket weaving. These Indian baskets are not only beautiful—they're strong and useful, too.

for woven shoulder bags. These *mochilas* are sometimes worn two or three at a time. The Guajiro Indians of the Guajira Peninsula sleep in woven hammocks. In colder climates, weavers turn out colorful woolen ruanas.

Hats are woven in a variety of styles. The most famous is the Panama hat. This broad-brimmed straw hat was first produced in Colombia in the early 1900s.

Besides the many gold objects, ceramics, and woven goods, Colombian artisans also create beautiful things out of wood, leather, beads, and feathers.

The "New" Arts

In Colombia, painting and literature are relatively new arts. They were introduced in the region by the Spanish, who arrived only 500 years ago.

COLOMBIA IN ARTS AND LETTERS

Jorge Isaacs (1837–1895) wrote only one novel, titled *Maria*, but it is the most popular romantic novel written in Spanish America. Besides its tale of doomed love, the novel contains beautiful descriptions of the Colombian countryside. Isaacs was passionately interested in writing. Unable to make a living as a writer, he took a number of government jobs, including one as a diplomat to Chile.

Jose Eustasio Rivera (1889–1928), poet and novelist, was born to a farming family. His parents made sure that their brilliant son got a good education. Rivera won fame for his novel *The Vortex*. It describes the mistreatment of rubber workers in the jungles of Colombia and Venezuela.

Alejandro Obregón (1920–1992) lived and worked in France during the late 1940s and early 1950s. There he came under the influence of the Spanish-born painter Pablo Picasso. Though Obregón is best known for his paintings of nature, many of his representations of human figures have a powerful political message. One is *Dead Student*, concerned with political violence in Colombia.

Gabriel García Márquez (1928–   ) spent his first eight years in the care of his maternal grandparents, who lived in an enormous house "full of ghosts." According to the writer, his grandparents were "people of great imagination and superstitions." His grandmother told terrifying stories that the boy nevertheless begged to hear because of their magic. García Márquez says that his grandmother's style of storytelling influenced his writing style.

This painting shows Fernando Botero's special artistic style.

Fernando Botero (1932–   ) is the son of a traveling salesman who died when the artist was a child. Although he studied in Europe, Botero was greatly influenced by Diego Rivera, the Mexican painter of murals. What Botero liked about Rivera's work was the combination of Indian and Spanish influences. Botero developed a unique style with human figures that all have the same kind of plump roundness.

With Pen . . .

The first Colombian writings were descriptions of the land and histories of its settlement by the Spanish. They were called chronicles. One popular chronicle, written by Juan Rodriguez Freile (1566–1640), told about the Spanish conquest. Freile called it *The Butcher*.

In the 1800s, Colombians favored poetry as a form of literary expression. Colombians still claim that more poets than military leaders have been presidents of their country. The poet–president Rafael Nuñez was responsible for Colombia's Constitution of 1886.

Today, Colombia is home to many fine writers. The most well known is Gabriel García Márquez. His books are a blend of realism and fantasy. He tells of events that could not possibly have happened. But he describes them with such realistic details that they seem true, at least in a symbolic way.

García Márquez's most famous work is *One Hundred Years of Solitude*. This is a tale of the people of the village of Macondo. This place is loosely based on the author's birthplace of Aracataca. For his many fine works of fiction, García Márquez won the Nobel Prize for Literature in 1982.

. . . and Brush

As long as Spain ruled Colombia, the paintings produced by Colombian artists reflected Spanish styles and trends. Most paintings were portraits of wealthy people or religious subjects. After Colombia won independence from Spain, local painters began to portray the customs, manners, and lifestyles of the people of Colombia. This artistic period was known as the *costumbrista* movement. One of the best-known artists of this movement was Ramón Torres Mendez.

More recently, two Colombian painters have won international fame. Alejandro Obregón, sometimes called the father of modern painting in Colombia, lived on the Caribbean coast. He took many of his images from the natural environment. His romantic seascapes are especially beloved. Fernando Botero, another famous Colombian artist, is known for the round shapes in his paintings. Sometimes he uses his style to poke fun at society and at people's weaknesses.

Making Music

No festival in Colombia is complete without music and dance. But Colombians don't limit their music-making to holidays. They do it all the time.

Colombian music comes from three different heritages: African, Indian, and Spanish. The African influence is felt most strongly on the coasts. There, the music is similar to that of the Caribbean islands and Central America. The marimba (a xylophone with wooden keys), drums, and maracas (gourds filled with seeds) help keep the lively Afro-Colombian beat going.

The more subdued strains of Indian music are heard in the mountains and in Amazonia. The sad tunes are made by instruments that have been played for centuries. The *flauta* is an Indian flute. The *tiple* is a many-stringed guitar. And the *raspa* is made from a gourd and played like a washboard.

The musical influence of the Spanish can be heard in soft ballads played on guitars.

Colombia's national dance—the *bambuco*—draws from all three of Colombia's musical heritages. One Colombian poet said the dance has Indian melancholy, African passion, and Andalusian (Spanish) courage. The *bambuco* is a "pursuit

Musicians in Cartagena play Afro-Colombian folk tunes called cumbias *on traditional instruments.*

dance" performed by a number of couples. At the beginning, each male partner pursues a woman until the two meet up. Then they continue the dance together. The *bambuco* musical beat resembles a waltz, but it has a quicker tempo.

The performance is fun to do—and to watch. Like Colombians themselves, the music and dance of Colombia are vigorous and lively, a celebration of life.

Country Facts

Official Name: República de Colombia (Republic of Colombia)

Capital: Bogotá (formally, Santa Fe de Bogotá)

Location: Colombia is located in the northern part of South America. It is bordered on the north by the Caribbean Sea, on the west by Panama and the Pacific Ocean, on the south by Ecuador and Peru, and on the east by Venezuela and Brazil.

Area: 440,831 square miles (1,141,748 kilometers). *Greatest distances:* northeast-southwest 850 miles (1,368 kilometers); northwest-southeast 1,170 miles (1,883 kilometers). *Coastline:* approximately 1,800 miles (2,880 kilometers)

Elevation: *Highest:* Cristóbal Colón peak in the Sierra Nevada of Santa Marta mountain, 18,947 feet (5,775 meters). *Lowest:* sea level, along the coast

Climate: There are a variety of climates. Temperature depends on elevation above sea level. Temperatures range from hot and humid on the coasts to cold and springlike in the mountains. Wet and dry seasons alternate.

Population: 36 million. *Distribution:* 73 percent urban; 27 percent rural

Form of Government: federal republic

Important Products: *Natural Resources:* coal, gold, emeralds, iron ore, natural gas, petroleum, salt. *Agriculture:* coffee, bananas, tropical fruits, flowers, sugarcane, potatoes, rice, beef cattle, corn, cotton. *Industries:* textiles, chemicals, cement, metal products, processed foods and beverages

Basic Unit of Money: peso; 1 peso = 100 centavos

Language: Spanish

Religion: About 95 percent of Colombians are Roman Catholics. There are also people who practice traditional Indian and African religions, mixed traditional and Christian faiths, Judaism, and Protestantism.

Flag: The Colombian flag has three horizontal stripes. The yellow (twice the size of the blue and red) symbolizes Colombia's wealth and resources. The blue represents its two oceans and many rivers. The red is a tribute to the patriots who fought for freedom from Spain.

National Anthems: *O Gloria Inmarcesible* and *Jubilo Inmortal* ("O Unwithering Glory" and "Immortal Joy")

Major Holidays: There are eighteen national holidays, and only six are not religious—New Year's Day (January 1), Labor Day (May 1), Independence Day (July 20), the Battle of Boyacá (August 7), Columbus Day (October 12), and the Independence of Cartagena (November 11). Important religious holidays include the Epiphany (January 6); Holy Thursday and Good Friday (in spring); the Assumption of the Virgin Mary (August 15); the Immaculate Conception (December 8); and Christmas (December 25).

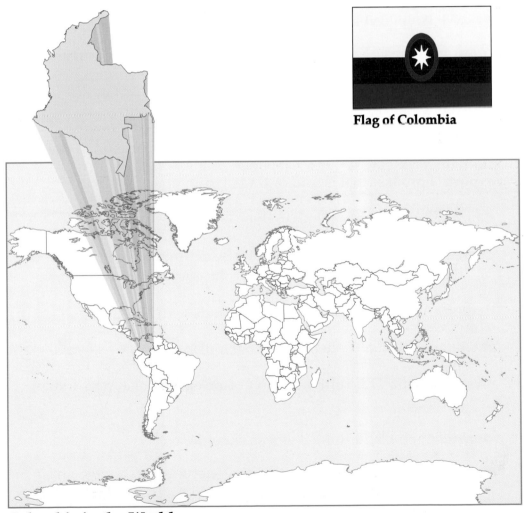

Flag of Colombia

Colombia in the World

Glossary

adobe (uh-DOH-bee): sun-dried brick

archaeologists (ahr-kee-OHL-oh-jist): people who learn about the past by digging up the remains of ancient cities and studying the tools, weapons, and pottery they find

arepas (ah-RAY-pahs): cornmeal pancakes, a favorite dish in Colombia

bambuco (bahm-BOO-koh): Colombia's national dance

compadrazgo (cohm-pah-DRAHZ-goh): co-parenting, or the special relationship between a child's parents and godparents

conquistadores: Spanish leaders who conquered the Indians in Mexico and South America

cordillera (kor-dee-YER-uh): a chain of mountains

Creole (KREE-ohl): a person of Spanish ancestry born in Colombia

export: a product that is sold or traded to another country

flauta (FLAOW-tuh): an Indian flute

guerrilla (ger-IL-uh): a member of a secret military organization that makes surprise raids to upset the government of a country

llanos (YAH-nohs): plains; grassy lowlands with few trees

mama: the spiritual leader of the Kogi Indians

mestizo (mehz-TEE-soh): a person of mixed Spanish and Indian heritage

mochila (moh-CHEE-luh): a woven shoulder bag

mulatto (muh-LAH-toh): a person of mixed African and European heritage

peninsula: a land area that is almost entirely surrounded by water

pre-Columbian: refers to the time before Europeans started exploring the Americas

raspa (RAHS-pah): an instrument that is made from a gourd and played like a washboard

ruana (roo-AH-nah): a cloak with a hole in the middle for the head to fit through

tiple (TEE-play): a many-stringed guitar

yucca: a plant with a nutritious starchy root that people can eat

zambo (ZAHM-boh): a person of mixed African and Indian heritage

For Further Reading

DuBois, Jill. *Colombia*. New York: Marshall Cavendish, 1991.

Haynes, Tricia. *Let's Visit Colombia*. London, England: Burke Publishing Company, 1985.

Jacobsen, Peter Otto, and Preben Sejer Kristensen. *A Family in Colombia*. New York: The Bookwright Press, 1986.

Morrison, Marion. *Colombia*. Chicago: Childrens Press, 1990.

Stewart, Gail. *Colombia*. New York: Crestwood House, 1991.

Sumwalt, Martha Murray. *Colombia in Pictures*. Minneapolis, Minnesota: Lerner Publications, 1993.

Vidal, Beatriz. *The Legend of El Dorado*. New York: Alfred A. Knopf, 1991.

Index

Page numbers for illustrations are in boldface

About the Author

Lois Markham graduated from Middlebury College in Vermont and taught high school English for a few years before becoming an editor at Scholastic. She has written numerous books for children, including biographies of Theodore Roosevelt, Thomas Edison, Helen Keller, and the authors Lois Lowry and Avi. She is a frequent contributor to *Kids Discover* magazine. In her spare time, Ms. Markham enjoys tap dancing and leading a Girl Scout troop. She lives in Beverly, Massachusetts, with her husband, Stephen Klesert, and their daughter, Amy.